THE BEGINNER'S GUIDE TO SELF-PUBLISHING A BOOK

A STEP-BY-STEP MANUAL

MICHAEL J HOLLEY

Copyright © 2014 by Michael J Holley

All rights reserved. This book or any portion thereof, in both printed or electronic form, may not be reproduced or used in any manner whatsoever without the express written permission of the publisher except for the use of brief quotations in a book review.

All characters, organisations and locations appearing in this work are fictitious. Any resemblance to real persons, living or dead, is purely coincidental.

ISBN 978-0-9575842-7-3

Cover design by James at GoOnWrite.com

First published in the United Kingdom in 2014 (1)

Beach Hut Publishing
Cowes
Isle of Wight

www.michaeljholley.com

You don't learn to walk by following rules.
You learn by doing, and by falling over.

Richard Branson

A Note from Scrivener

"We first became aware of 'Michael J Holley – Writer' through our company Twitter feed. Michael was penning extremely useful Scrivener related blog posts, which we enthusiastically retweeted.

We're now delighted to see that Michael has written "The Beginner's Guide to Self-Publishing a Book – A Step-by-Step Manual" that does exactly as the title suggests!

Many thanks to Michael for detailing all the steps required, whilst using Scrivener, for self-publishing authors to achieve their goal."

Contents

Introduction	9
Section 1 - Getting Started	
Why should you self-publish?	15
What is self-publishing?	22
The process of self-publishing	27
Process Tick Sheet	29
Software and Tools	31
Required material	35
Section 2 - Scrivener	
Create a new document	41
Transfer from a word processor	43
Using the Corkboard	45
Full Screen Composition Mode	47
Target Tracker	49
Inserting Images	51
Inserting the Cover Design	53
Syncing with Other Devices	55
Section 3 - Professional Editing	
Professional Editing	59
Section 4 - Preparing the Manuscript	
The Interior Design	65
Fiction Design Example	67
Non-Fiction Design Example	71
Build the Right Structure	75
Page settings	77
Formatting	81

  Front Matter 85
  Adding a Contents Page 91
  Back Matter 93
Section 5 - Cover Design
  Cover Design 99
Section 6 - Creating a Product Description
  Creating a product description 107
Section 7 - ISBNs
  ISBNs 115
Section 8 - Compiling the Manuscript
  Compiling an eBook File 121
  Reviewing an eBook File 127
  Compiling a Paperback File 131
  Reviewing a Paperback File 141
Section 9 - Publishing the eBook
  Publishing to Amazon 147
  Publishing to Smashwords 155
Section 10 - Publishing The Paperback
  Publishing to CreateSpace 161
Section 11 - Next Steps
  Next Steps 169
Note from the author 173
Author resources 175
Acknowledgements 177

Introduction

Hi, and welcome to 'The Beginner's Guide to Self-Publishing a Book: A Step-by-Step Manual'.

Before I explain to you in a greater number of words that this book is simply a practical manual for how to produce a professional-looking book for yourself, I thought it would be polite to introduce myself first. My name's Michael, I've been a full-time writer since 2011 and I've been absorbed in self-publishing for longer still.

Although I love to help people learn how to publish for themselves via my blog, courses and books, my first love is being a writer. I want to be able to spend as much time as I can writing, and that's why I want to clarify the process of self-publishing for you, so that you can spend more time writing as well.

There are already so many books on the market which discuss the benefits and tactics of self-publishing, rather than the actual nuts and bolts of *how* to self-publish. The purpose of this book is to give you the tools and knowledge to do it yourself.

It's a manual for self-publishing.

Within these pages, I'll go through the entire process for how to transform your manuscript into a published book. There are obviously a thousand ways to format a book but, as you're primarily a writer, the most important goal is to confidently publish a professional looking book, as quickly and as easily as possible, so that you can then move on to the next one.

> *"It's not done until it ships..."* - Steve Jobs

The entire purpose of writing a book, be it fiction or non-fiction, is for others to read it. For so long, the publishing industry has restricted that goal from being achieved, but now the rules have changed. Self-publishing is rapidly becoming the largest route to market due to the popularity of ebooks, the development in printing technology, and the freedom that it gives to the author. All of this together is creating a revolution in the publishing world and the more popular it gets, the less of a stigma the term 'self-publishing' holds.

Let's be clear straightaway, I'm not talking about Vanity Publishing (the term traditionally given to publications for which authors would pay for the production themselves). There's nothing false about self-publishing. It's not an ego trip for a terrible writer who can temporarily delude himself. Self-publishing is a viable business model and is becoming a realistic approach for any new author.

However, there is one important characteristic which self-published books must adhere to...

...they must be comparable in every way to a professionally published book.

What's the point of throwing something online which looks like a school project? The playing field has been levelled, those evil gate-keepers have been banished, and now your success is in your own hands.

This book will tell you exactly what you need to do in order to produce a professional looking product. Although self-publishing is all about freedom of expression, we're not all blessed with a keen eye for design or technical expertise. These obstacles shouldn't prevent you from making your book appear as professional as it can or from even attempting to publish in the first place.

As a self-published author of fiction, I'm obsessed with streamlining the process which I, myself, have to go through. Each step is meticulously laid out in the following chapters and I recommend you keep this on your desk so that you can constantly refer to it as needed. I've discovered most of the information by painstakingly searching websites within the self-publishing community, plus the time consuming technique known as 'trial and error'. This book will be your short-cut.

I want to encourage you to self-publish. I want you to achieve your publishing goals and I want you to be proud of your work by the end of it.

So, let's start publishing and... good luck...

1

Getting Started

Why Should You Self-Publish?

Before we start learning *how* to self-publish, we should probably convince ourselves that this is, without a shadow of a doubt, the most beneficial, reasonable and appropriate course of action open to us.

Why not?

You may have some long-standing beliefs about self-publishing which I'd like to quash right now. Here are some of the common misconceptions:

- It's the last resort of the untalented writer
- It's known as vanity publishing
- It's expensive
- I won't be able to sell any copies
- I'll be ripped off by a publishing conman
- I'll be laughed at by people
- Real authors get published traditionally
- I'm better than this
- Authors are meant to struggle for their art

- If I self-publish then I'll ruin my chances of ever getting traditionally published
- I'll earn more money if I sign a publishing contract
- I'll receive better promotion with a publisher
- My book will appear in bookshops with a publisher
- I don't like ebooks and that's all that self-publishing is
- This is just fashionable at the moment

I assume, because you've bought this book, that you must at least be intrigued by self-publishing. Let me explain a little about how self-publishing has changed and how the publishing industry has changed around it.

The self-publishing revolution

When Amazon released its first Kindle eReader at the end of 2007, they also introduced a new tool, Kindle Direct Publishing (KDP), which enabled authors to publish books on the Amazon platform for themselves. Hence, the publishing revolution began.

Amazon offered authors a 70% royalty which compared to a traditional publishers 10-20%, and also coupled with the benefit of zero barriers to entry, pioneering authors began to embrace the new opportunity. Ebooks were a controversial addition back then and the industry passed through a period of denial, conflict and adjustment.

Self-publishing requires no middle-men anymore. You know

the guys who set themselves up as small publishers to take exorbitant amounts of money off of authors just to publish their books for them. They're not needed anymore. You can do it yourself, for free.

The growth of ebooks

Another home truth to get your head around is that ebooks are here to stay. Volume and sales have increased rapidly since their introduction and 2013 figures have ebooks now making up 25% of the total market. As more people own eReaders this figure will continue to grow. PriceWaterhouseCoopers estimate that by 2018 ebooks will overtake the printed form.

Although this is a statistic shared by both self-publishers as well as the traditionally published, it translates to a lot more freedom for authors. In the old days, to buy a printed book used to mean having it out there in the bookshops and then promoting it like a wild man until its shelf-life evaporated, at which point it would disappear, maybe never to see the light of day again. Shelf space in bookshops was owned by the big publishers because that was the eco-system they operated in. This was a pretty rough deal for any author.

Firstly, you had to be one of the lucky few percent who would be published in the first place but, if you'd achieved this, then came the next part. If you were still lucky then the publisher would pay for you to appear cover up on one of the tables as you walk into a bookshop. However, this would only last for about a month at most until you were relegated to a spine out placement on one of the many shelves, eventually disappearing with a whimper. The publisher would then be likely to drop you because your book didn't sell enough.

Ebooks have changed all of this. Firstly, ebooks never die, they'll never go out of print; secondly, a self-published author can stand side by side with an author from, let's say Penguin, and have the same chance of success; thirdly, a self-published author will make up to 60% more per ebook than her traditionally published peer.

I'm not just talking about selling books locally either. You can now find readers from anywhere in the world, you can build a fan base and furnish them directly with your products. This is the modern world and we live in a globalised marketplace where you can connect with your readers in a hundred different ways.

Print-on-demand

The story isn't just about ebooks either. Since digital printing technology has developed, it's now possible to run a single-book print run. This is called Print-On-Demand and it means that self-publishers can now sell printed books for no initial cost. The days of cardboard boxes, filled with books, piled high in a garage are over.

Improved chance of success

All of these factors have forced the traditional publishers, with their high overheads, to change their operations. They've stopped taking so many chances with new authors because they simply can't afford the risk; celebrity biographies, cookbooks and best-selling authors are their bread and butter now. The lottery of the slush pile has only worsened for new authors and instead, the online charts have become the new filtering method.

There are many examples now of authors who have begun by self-publishing, achieved success on their own terms and have since signed more appealing traditional contracts. Examples of these authors are; EL James (author of Fifty Shades of Grey), Hugh Howey (author of the Wool series) and Nick Spalding (author of the Love series). The argument that self-publishing will jeopardise an author's chances for a traditional contract is no longer true and instead, there's even evidence that it improves them.

AuthorEarnings.com

Hugh Howey, one of the most successful self-publishers in the last few years, has been passionately convincing other writers of the benefits to self-publishing. Along with a statistician who has mined Amazon for readable data, he has proven that self-published authors now earn more money as a whole than if they were published by any other means. The graph below shows his findings from July 2014:

Daily $ Revenue To Authors from e-Book Bestsellers
(120,000 books comprising ~50% of Amazon e-Book revenue)
(Fiction and Nonfiction - July 14, 2014)

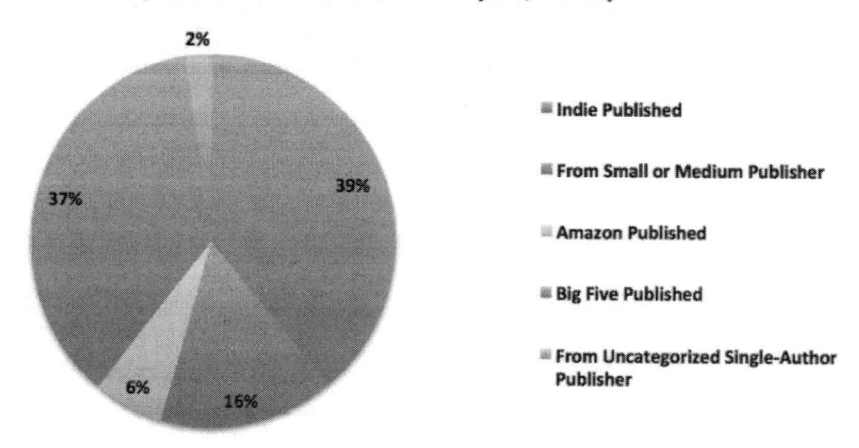

- Indie Published — 39%
- From Small or Medium Publisher — 6%
- Amazon Published — 2%
- Big Five Published — 37%
- From Uncategorized Single-Author Publisher — 16%

This graph has been kindly taken from AuthorEarnings.com

Freedom of self-publishing

So, apart from the industry changing, the ebook revolution, and the favourable royalty rate, why else would you want to self-publish? The answer should be pretty obvious. The benefit of self-publishing is that you're the boss. You can choose which books you want to write, you can decide how many books you'll release a year, you can select the best cover for your book, be in control of your author branding, pricing, marketing and everything else.

There's no need to wait until you find the right sort of publisher, who is looking for the right type of book, at the right time you ask them. You can publish it yourself and move on with the next one. Life's too short to play the waiting game. Wouldn't it be better to reach out and find your readers directly? For the first time in the history of marking pieces of paper with words, it's now possible for anyone to make a living as a writer. The only thing stopping you right now is your own ability to start publishing your work.

So, let's do something about that...

What Is Self-Publishing?

By now, you should be champing at the bit to get started but, just before we do, maybe it's a good idea to clarify exactly what we mean by self-publishing.

The traditional definition:

"Self-publishing is the publication of any book or other media by the author of the work, without the involvement of an established third-party publisher."

However, I think I should clarify this in more detail so that we completely understand each other. This is what I mean when I refer to self-publishing, or indeed the newer term, indie-publishing.

Creation of ebooks

It was the ebook which made the revolution possible. It's cheap and efficient to distribute to anyone with an eReader, a tablet or a smart phone. In this book, I will explain exactly how to produce a professional looking ebook.

Creation of paperbacks

A print-on-demand paperback version of your book is free to set up and I'll show you how to create and submit the appropriate files which will link directly to Amazon. Some believe that paperbacks are not as effective for the self-publisher but, a benefit of selling them next to your ebooks is that your book will look more professional if it's available in multiple formats.

Professional quality

Just because you're self-publishing doesn't mean that you can throw up on to a page and publish it, hoping for the best. The self-published books which look as though they've been put together during a party, thankfully, tend to disappear from view pretty fast. You must aim to produce a book which can be compared with a product created by a traditional publisher who's been doing it for a hundred years. They have a fair amount of experience and they should be copied as much as possible. I'll be exploring cover design in more detail later but, you should also have your work professionally edited before ever releasing it into the wild.

Author Branding

What I mean by 'author branding' is the image you want to put across to your readers. There's usually a whole department of people looking at this for a traditionally published author and it shows. This type of thing looks professional and remember, that's what you're trying to achieve. Your image is important and it must be consistent whilst evoking the appropriate response.

Marketing

You're in charge of how your books are going to be marketed, where they'll be available and how much they'll cost. All promotions are up to you and the experimentation which occurs on the marketing side is a great sharing point across the entire self-publishing community. In this dynamic sub-industry, promotional vehicles are changing all of the time and a strategy which worked a year ago will soon become obsolete.

The Self-Publishing Process

This manual will describe the process shown on the next page. This is certainly the most popular approach to self-publishing. There are other approaches available but, by using this method, you can be confident of publishing a quality product, which will subsequently be available on all major online book retailing sites, as both an ebook and a paperback, and will enable you to get on with your next project with the minimum amount of fuss.

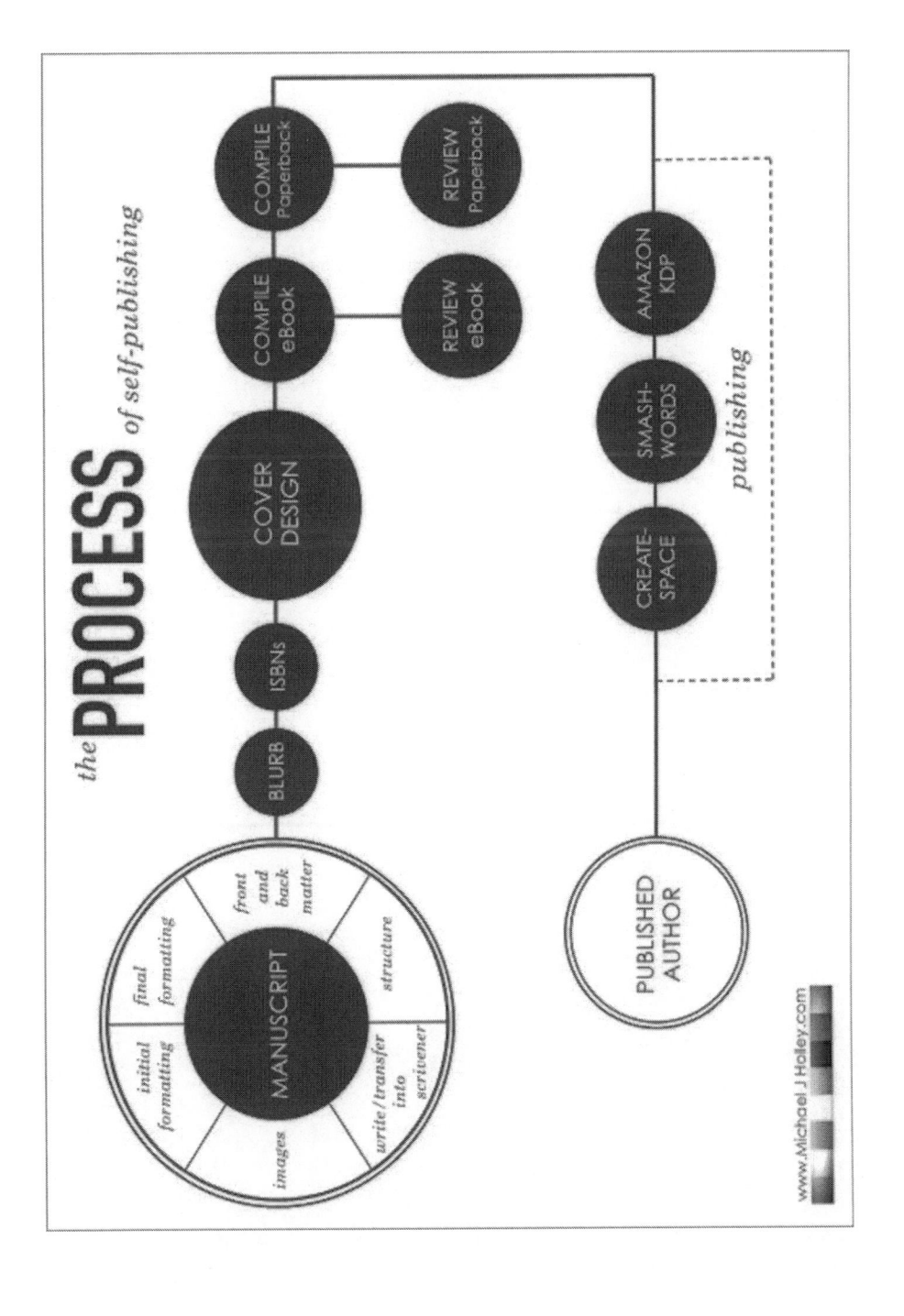

the PROCESS *of self-publishing*

MANUSCRIPT
- initial formatting
- final formatting
- front and back matter
- structure
- write / transfer into scrivener
- images

BLURB → ISBNs → COVER DESIGN → COMPILE eBook → COMPILE Paperback

REVIEW eBook

REVIEW Paperback

publishing
CREATESPACE → SMASHWORDS → AMAZON KDP

PUBLISHED AUTHOR

www.MichaelJHolley.com

the PROCESS *of self-publishing*

Manuscript — 1
- [ ] First Draft
- [ ] Second Draft
- [ ] Beta-Readers
- [ ] Third Draft
- [ ] Professional Editor
- [ ] Final Draft

Cover Design — 2
- [ ] Brief submitted
- [ ] eBook .jpeg file received
- [ ] Paperback .jpeg file rec'd

ISBN — 3
- [ ] ISBN's allocated

Blurb — 4
- [ ] First Draft
- [ ] Final Draft

.mobi & .epub files — 5
- [ ] Page Settings
- [ ] Formatting
- [ ] Front Matter
- [ ] Back Matter
- [ ] Contents Page
- [ ] Images
- [ ] Compile

Paperback .pdf file — 6
- [ ] Page Settings
- [ ] Formatting
- [ ] Front Matter
- [ ] Back Matter
- [ ] Contents Page
- [ ] Images
- [ ] Compile

Publishing — 7
- [ ] Published to KDP
- [ ] Published to Smashwords
- [ ] Published to CreateSpace

Software and Tools

Before you get started, you need to make sure that you're familiar with the tools you're going to use.

1 Software

Scrivener
Outline. Edit. Storyboard. *Write.*

Scrivener is a powerful content-generation tool designed especially for writers, which will not only allow you to complete your manuscript as efficiently as possible but, it then packages it up in the necessary publishable formats. This is where it sets itself apart from other simple word processing tools and the time it will save you is worth the extremely modest investment.

I recommend you use this tool even if you've written your manuscript in Microsoft Word. It'll take away any pain that may result from having to use other software to create your ebook files.

Scrivener can be downloaded at www.literatureandlatte.com/scrivener.php

2 Free download

Kindle Previewer

This is used to review the Kindle ebook file before publication.

(www.amazon.com/gp/feature.html?docId=1000765261)

Calibre

This is used to review the Smashwords ebook file before publication.

(www.calibre-ebook.com)

PDF File Viewer, such as Adobe Reader

This is used to review the paperback file before publication.

(www.get.adobe.com/uk/reader)

3 Web-based

Kindle Direct Publishing (KDP)

KDP is the website which enables you to publish your ebook in the largest bookshop in the world. The actual publishing upload process is surprisingly simple.

(www.kdp.amazon.com)

Smashwords

This is where you can upload your ebook in order for it to be distributed to all other major ebook retailers, including Apple, Kobo, and Barnes & Noble.

(www.smashwords.com)

CreateSpace

This is the most popular print-on-demand facility commonly used by self-publishers. It's a subsidiary of Amazon and is therefore directly linked to the Amazon store.

(www.createspace.com)

Required Material

In order to self-publish your book, as both an ebook and a paperback online, you will require certain files and information to facilitate the upload process.

1. .mobi file for ebooks available on Amazon
2. .epub file for ebooks available elsewhere
3. .jpeg file of ebook cover design
4. .pdf file of paperback cover design
5. A product description
6. An ISBN number (maybe)

Once you have all six components, you will be ready to self-publish.

1 .mobi file for ebooks available on Amazon

The .mobi file can be produced from Scrivener in the exact format you require to upload into Amazon's KDP website. It can only be used for the direct purpose of uploading to Amazon and it contains all of your ebook data which will eventually feature on an eReader, including the cover image and contents.

2 .epub file for ebooks available elsewhere

The .epub file can be used to upload into Smashwords. Smashwords, in turn, will distribute your book to all other major online book retailers, including Apple's iBookstore, Kobo, and Barnes & Noble. Similar to the .mobi file, it holds all of your ebook's data.

3 .jpeg file of ebook cover design

One of the benefits of using a professional cover designer, as I recommend, is that they will provide you with the necessary files in the appropriate formats to upload.

If you choose another route then you will still require a .jpeg image file. For the ebook, you only require the front cover image. It must also be in a high resolution format.

4 .pdf file of paperback cover design

For the print-on-demand paperback, you require a .pdf image file showing the complete wrap around cover, including any back of book text, barcode, publisher's imprint, etc.

5 a product description

All online websites require you to provide a product description for your project. This must be entered at the time of publishing.

6 an ISBN number

This stands for the International Standard Book Number. It is a mechanism for officially registering a book with your national library, improving its discoverability and enhancing its physical sales potential. However, it is not mandatory and in Section 6 I will discuss both sides of the decision.

2

Scrivener Guide

Create a New Document

When opening Scrivener, firstly create your project.

1 The 'Project Templates' box appears with options for Fiction, Non-Fiction, Scriptwriting and Poetry.

FICTION:

Select Fiction/Novel

Within this Project Template, there are sections created specifically for the fiction writer, such as; Characters, Places, Front Matter, and Research. You are able to store all of the background information you have collected for your novel in one place, so that it's easy to get your hands on.

NON-FICTION:

Select Non-Fiction/General Non-Fiction

Within this Project Template, there are sections created specifically for the non-fiction writer, such as; Foreword, Contents, Ideas and Research.

2 Save the project with a suitable name and you can begin.

Transfer from a Word Processor

You may have already written your manuscript, or at least started writing it, in a word processor such as Microsoft Word or Open Office. If you have then don't fear; there's a quick and efficient way to transfer your existing file into Scrivener.

Your existing document will be one continuous manuscript. You may have page breaks for each chapter, or section, but overall it will scroll as one continuous piece of writing. One of Scrivener's strengths is that you can split your book into the relevant sections and the sections will be identified by a typical folder structure. When you transfer your existing document to Scrivener, you can elect to 'Split' it at the appropriate points and it will create the necessary folder structure to support your project.

1 Save your existing file

2 In Scrivener, Select File/Import/Files... and choose the appropriate file

3 Your existing document will become a 'Scene' or a text file within the Binder structure on the left-hand side.

4 You'll then need to split the document up into its separate sections. You can do this by leaving the cursor at the beginning of the new section and then selecting Documents/Split/at Selection, or right clicking and selecting 'Split at Selection'.

5 Your document is now split up in to a number of separate scenes, or text files, on the left-hand side of the Binder. In Section 4, I'll explain how to create the appropriate file structure for your book and how to move these text files into chapters.

Using the Corkboard

There's nothing now stopping you from ploughing on and creating your magnum opus but, before you do, there are a couple of handy tools within Scrivener's broad compendium of writing aids which you might find useful. The first of these is the corkboard functionality.

Some degree of planning is essential when writing a book and instead of using Post-It notes on a wall in your office, why not use the corkboard in Scrivener itself.

1 Access the corkboard by selecting View/Corkboard, or the corkboard icon at the top

2 Right click, then Add/New Folder, or Text, and an index card is created. (Notice that this is reflected in the Binder structure on the left-hand side)

3 Write text either directly on to the card by double-clicking or by using the synopsis box in top right-hand corner.

4 Cards can then be moved around limitlessly and their structure will be replicated in the structure of your book.

* If you follow the 'story beats' methodology, or the 'snowflake method', either can be accommodated by the corkboard by writing the detail of the chapter straight on to the index card. This can then be left on display when writing the content for the specific passage.

Full Screen Composition Mode

The common enemy for writers is distraction. It raises its head and stops you from getting into flow. In the past, I've tried writing on the tops of mountains and at the bottom of the sea, but I still can't avoid distraction. However, when writing at your computer the major distraction these days is the internet, and of course email, lurking seductively at the edge of your screen, horrible little notifications appearing from nowhere.

Scrivener has the answer for this and it's called Full Screen Composition mode.

1 Access the full screen mode by selecting View/Enter Composition Mode, or by using the icon at the top of the screen. As soon as you do, the world as you know it disappears and all you're left with is a black screen and a page. All notifications are suspended and temptation is banished.

2 Display settings can be changed by moving the pointer down to the bottom of the screen.

3 The synopsis can be displayed by selecting the Inspector, and also word targets can be displayed if they have already been selected before changing to composition mode.

Target Tracker

During the arduous process of creating our manuscript, us writers fall back on various devices to simply get the words down on the page. One of the most common methods we employ is a daily word count. Of course, Scrivener has realised this and has provided a tool just for the job.

1 Access the targets by selecting Project/Show Project Targets.

2 There are two options; the total manuscript target and the session target. You can set each of these by double-clicking the value, making a change and selecting Apply. You can also decide at which point the session target will reset, by selecting the Options.

* If you're using the Full Screen writing mode then remember to open up your targets first before changing to Full Screen, the targets box will then stay on top when everything else disappears.

Inserting Images

The ability to insert images into your manuscript is essential, especially for non-fiction books, however you must be aware of increasing your digital delivery costs. The more images your ebook file holds, the larger the file size will be. Amazon, as an example, will charge a delivery cost for an ebook based on $0.15 per megabyte, so keeping your digital file smaller will provide you with a greater flexibility later with pricing.

You should convert any images to the most optimum resolution size before inserting them into your document. 200dpi is a benchmark set by CreateSpace.

Please be aware though, eBooks are not that great at consistently displaying images. Even within the Kindle family, images appear differently across the various devices. You will need to review your digital files before publishing to ensure that they display appropriately.

1 Insert images by leaving the cursor in the correct place in your manuscript and then selecting Edit/Insert/Image From File...

2 Browse to the appropriate file and select Open.

3 In order to scale the image to the appropriate size for paperbacks, double-click on the image and move the pointer along the ruler until it's right. Alternatively, for eBooks, I've found that setting the left value to 750 will look best across most devices.

4 To ensure that all images are aligned centrally, select Format/Text/Center.

5 Remove any First-Line Indentation by selecting Format/Text/Increase/Decrease Indents/Decrease First Line Indent. (Note: you may have to do this a few times depending on how many indents you have)

Inserting Cover Design

The cover is probably the most important aspect of your book, it's the shop window and it's the biggest reason why anyone will ever want to take a closer look at it. Getting the image into your ebook is therefore quite an important part of the process.

I'll be exploring how to go about designing your cover in Section 2, but for now let's just take a look at how you can actually insert it within the Scrivener project. It actually depends on whether you created your Scrivener manuscript using a non-fiction format template, or a fiction format template.

1. Fiction format template

1 Highlight the sub-folder called 'E-Book' within the folder called Front Matter. The folder will already be there as a placeholder within the fiction template Binder.

2 Once highlighted, select File/Import/Files...

3 Browse through your files and select the .jpeg image you require

2. Non-Fiction format template

1 Highlight 'Non-Fiction Format' at the very top of the binder on the left-hand side

2 Select File/Import/Files...

3 Browse through your files and select the .jpeg image you require

Syncing with Other Devices

One of the greatest privileges of being a writer is the ability to work from anywhere but, it's a challenge sometimes to always have your computer with you. So far, the Scrivener team have been unable to release a mobile app which can be used on a mobile device, so we have a problem. How can you continue to edit and add to your document whilst being away from the office?

The answer is certainly not as effective as a specific app but, once set up, it's still relatively automatic.

1 Install the free Textilus app on your mobile device

2 Register for a free Dropbox account and follow the instructions to set it up on your computer

3 Create a folder within your new Dropbox folder for writing and then a sub-folder for your current project.

4 Select File/Sync/with External Folder...

5 Link the newly created folder in the Dropbox folder to Scrivener by choosing it in the 'Shared Folder' to sync files from this project.

6 Keep all other settings the same and select Sync.

7 Open Textilus on your mobile device, link your Dropbox folder and then navigate to the specific folder to find your Scrivener project.

8 Textilus will sync automatically when you close a document and Scrivener will also sync automatically when you close Scrivener. If you'd rather sync from Scrivener without closing it then select File/Sync/with External Folder Now.

3

Professional Editing

Professional Editing

Self-publishing does not mean that you should attempt everything on your own. Self-publishing means that you have the freedom to do everything a traditional publisher does, but better.

It's impossible for a writer to edit their own work effectively, even if they're a professional editor themselves. Editing requires an element of objectivity, which is unattainable if you've spent the last six months staring at every sentence.

You can secure the services of a professional editor simply by searching the internet for book editing services. The cost is usually somewhere between $800 and $2-3,000, depending on detail and experience.

There are a number of different edits which you can outsource:

High-level edit / Developmental edit

This type of edit means that the editor will work with the author to craft the manuscript, looking at structure and argument in non-fiction or plot and character in fiction. They are often used near the beginning of the process.

Line edit

This type of edit looks at the manuscript as a whole and makes corrections based on each individual line. This is a much more detailed edit but less personal.

Copy edit

The copy edit applies to the overall theme of the project and makes sure that it is consistent with itself. It ensures the continuity, the formatting, the accuracy but is unlikely to change the content of the text.

Proofread

The proofread will literally go through every single sentence and correct for grammar and spelling mistakes. This will eliminate the dreaded typo which haunts every author's dreams.

Beta-readers

Another important role which shouldn't be under-estimated is that of the beta-reader. It's typical for a beta-reader to receive a second draft version and to then comment on the high-level themes within the book, such as plot, character, and flow. Beta-readers tend to be free and are often friends of the writer, or people simply willing to help.

4

Preparing the Manuscript

The Interior Design

In order to prepare the manuscript for publishing, there are a number of steps which must be followed. There are two reasons why I recommend using Scrivener; firstly, it's commonly regarded as the best writing software on the market; but secondly, it enables you to create the required files from your manuscript which will be needed later in the process.

The files which are produced from Scrivener are:

- .mobi file (Amazon Kindle Format)
- .epub file (Other eBook Format)
- .pdf file (Paperback Format)

In order to create the best looking end product, it's important to remember that we are aiming to achieve a professional and high quality result.

In the next chapter, I've included an example of both a fiction and a non-fiction interior design. The subsequent chapters in this section will then explain *how* to recreate the look for yourself.

Obviously, design is subjective and everyone will have different tastes. You can follow the guidelines in this section and be confident of producing a quality looking book, or you can select different options based on your own preferences. Each chapter will show you the method and, once you have this knowledge, you are free to use it as you choose.

One of the benefits of self-publishing is the creative freedom that it gives us as writers, but I would always balance this with the lessons that we can learn from traditionally published work. Before deciding on the interior design of your book, I advise you to research your genre and other favourite books, to give you ideas.

> *"Good artists copy but great artists steal..."* - Pablo Picasso

These are the components that make up the interior design:

- Build the right structure
- Page Settings
- Formatting
- Front Matter
- Adding a contents page
- Back matter

Example of Fiction Formatting

These are examples of a standard, professional, fiction format which you can produce for yourself. This section will describe exactly how to replicate this interior design from within Scrivener.

The screenshots are from the paperback version but the ebook format will look similar. eReaders manipulate the formatting of ebook files in order to produce a generic, standard format and this limits the amount of specific formatting which is possible.

Title page

Michael J Holley

Copyright and Dedication pages

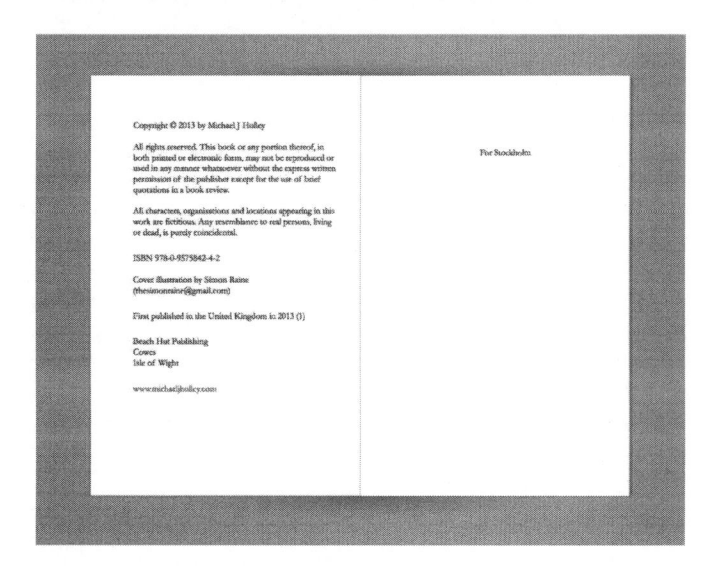

Beginning of Chapter page

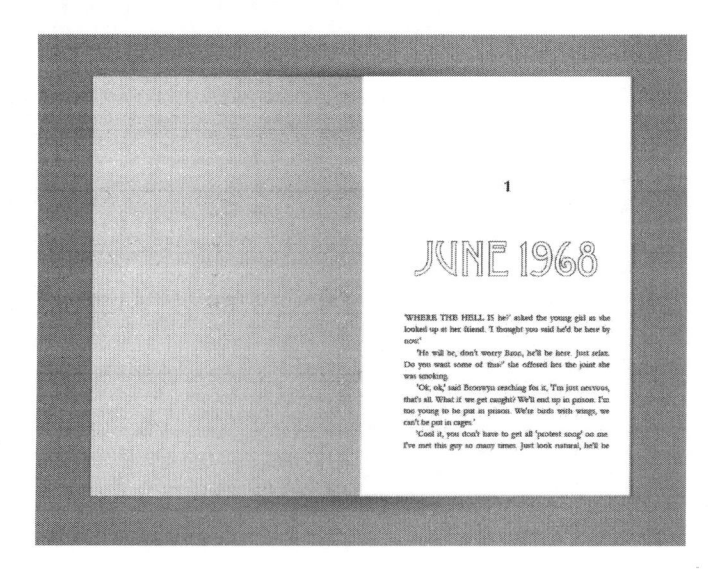

Mid-chapter pages

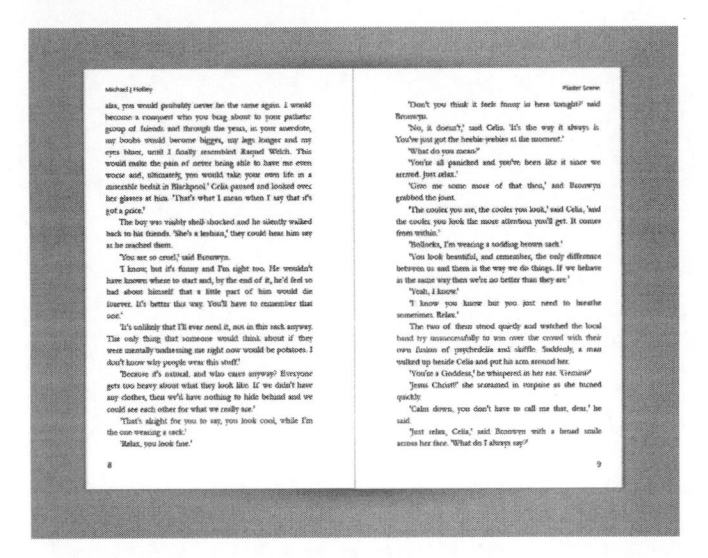

(Note: the headers and footers will be different in the ebook file)

Mid-chapter pages

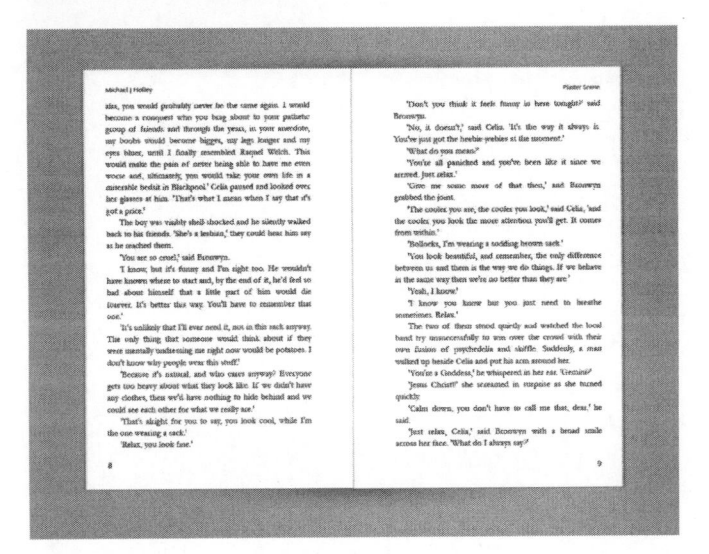

(Note: the headers and footers will be different in the ebook file)

Example of Non-Fiction Formatting

These are examples of a standard, professional, non-fiction format which you can produce for yourself. This section will describe exactly how to replicate this interior design from within Scrivener.

The screenshots are from the paperback version but the ebook format will look similar. eReaders manipulate the formatting of ebook files in order to produce a generic, standard format and this limits the amount of specific formatting which is possible.

Section page

Images and Sub-headings

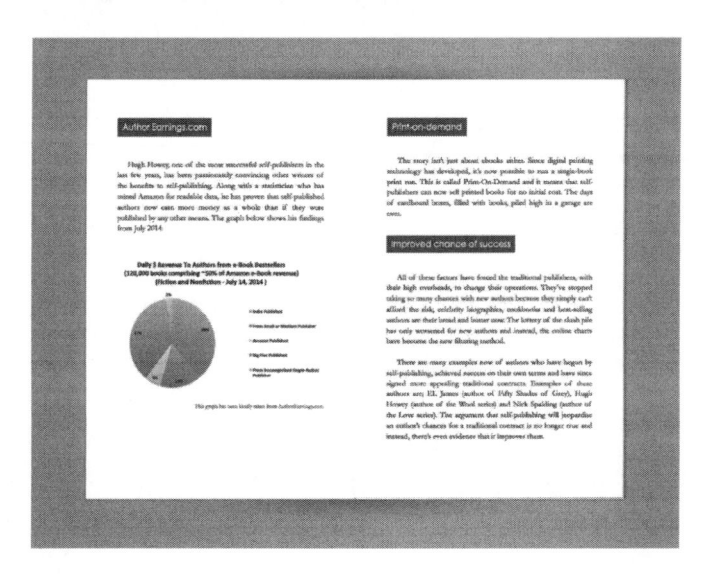

Tables

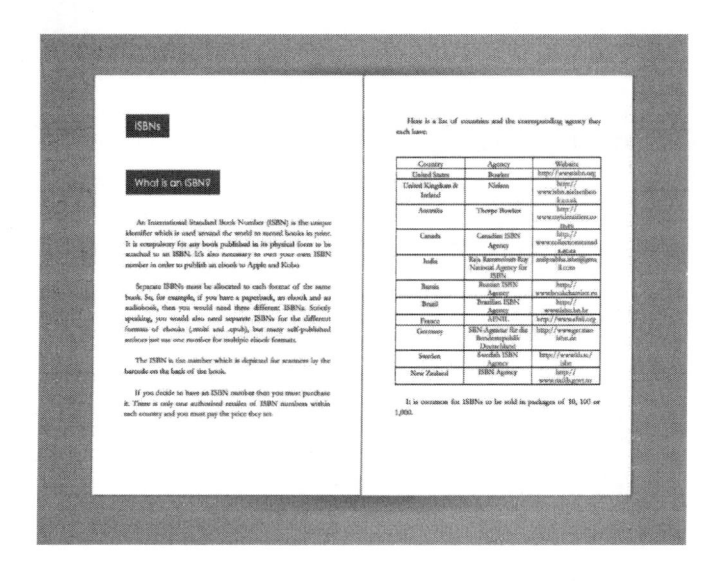

Diagrams

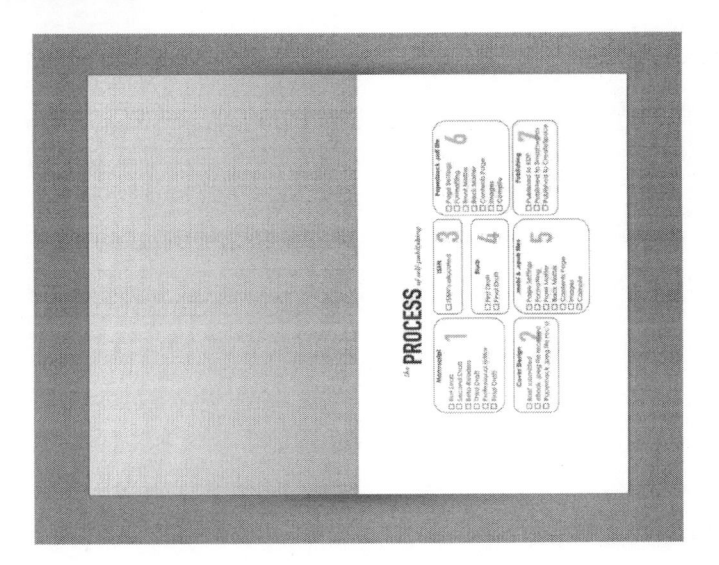

Build the Right Structure

Within Scrivener, the 'Binder' does the job of a big, leather-bound compendium in real life. You can write scenes and keep them separate from each other, endlessly rearranging them until your project makes sense.

The 'Binder' runs down the left-hand side of the page and looks like any other typical folder hierarchy. A folder exists at the top which has either other folders, or text files, linking into it. The text file is always at the bottom of that specific leg of the hierarchy. For example, you could have the following:

Manuscript

- Section 1 (Folder)
    - Chapter 1 (Folder)
        - Scene 1 (Text File)
        - Scene 2 (Text File)
    - Chapter 2 (Folder)
        - Scene 3 (Text File)
- Section 2 (Folder)
    - Scene 4 (Text File)

The levels in the hierarchy are infinitely changeable and you can create the specific structure which your project requires. You don't need to know the eventual structure at the beginning because you'll be able to adjust it throughout the life of the project. It's very simple to create new levels within the 'Binder'.

1 Right-click anywhere within the hierarchy and select Add/New Text or New Folder, this will create a new extension directly below where you have highlighted.

2 You can also drag levels of the hierarchy to other areas by left-clicking, holding and moving to the desired area.

Page Settings

Once you have created the necessary structure, I recommend you set up the page view in Scrivener to mirror the eventual paperback format. Not only does this make the paperback easier to compile but it also helps when compiling the ebook too. It will also give you an indicator, whilst writing, of how many pages you've produced.

This is a table of the standard book sizes which are produced by CreateSpace, the print-on-demand supplier.

5 x 8 inches, 12.7 x 20.32 centimeters
5.06 x 7.81 inches, 12.9 x 19.8 centimeters
5.25 x 8 inches, 13.335 x 20.32 centimeters
5.5 x 8.5 inches, 13.97 x 21.59 centimeters
6 x 9 inches, 15.24 x 22.86 centimeters
6.14 x 9.21 inches, 15.6 x 23.4 centimeters
6.69 x 9.61 inches, 17 x 24.4 centimeters
7 x 10 inches, 17.78 x 25.4 centimeters
7.44 x 9.69 inches, 18.9 x 24.6 centimeters
7.5 x 9.25 inches, 19.1 x 23.5 centimeters
8 x 10 inches, 20.32 x 25.4 centimeters
8.25 x 6 inches, 20.955 x 15.24 centimeters
8.25 x 8.25 inches, 20.955 x 20.955 centimeters
8.5 x 11 inches, 21.59 x 27.94 centimeters
8.5 x 8.5 inches, 21.59 x 21.59 centimeters

For fiction, I use the standard UK trade paperback B-format size (5.06" x 7.81"); and for non-fiction, I use a standard format (6.14" x 9.21"), both highlighted on the previous page.

This is how to change the page settings in Scrivener:

1 Select File/Page Setup...

2 Ensure the Settings drop-down is showing 'Page Attributes', Select the Paper Size drop down and select Manage Custom Sizes...

3 To replicate the examples at the beginning of this section, enter the following values:

		Fiction	Non-Fiction
Paper Size:	Width	129mm	156mm
	Height	198mm	234mm
	Top	7mm	10mm
	Bottom	9mm	15mm
	Left	10mm	18mm
	Right	10mm	18mm

The Beginner's Guide to Self-Publishing A Book

4 Then change the Settings drop down to 'Scrivener' and enter the following values:

	Fiction	Non-Fiction
Top	1.4cm	2.2cm
Bottom	1.7cm	2.2cm
Left	2.0cm	1.9cm
Right	1.0cm	1.9cm

(Note: the reason these two sets of values are different is due to the placement of the header and page numbers. The Paper Size refers to the entire content on the page, whereas the Scrivener values refer to just the writing content.)

5 To make sure that these settings are reflected within the 'Page View' in Scrivener. Select the root menu Scrivener/Preferences. On the Editor tab, check at the bottom that '"Printed Page Size" uses' is showing 'File>Page Setup settings'.

Formatting

Font

The formatting of the text is only relevant to the paperback. Ereaders either use a generic font, like Times New Roman, or they allow the reader to choose from a limited selection.

I prefer to use the eventual font when writing, so I make sure the settings are correct before I start.

1 Select the root menu Scrivener/Preferences and then go to the Formatting tab.

2 To replicate the fiction example at the beginning of this section, change the Main Text Style font to Garamond 12.

(Note: this is obviously a subjective preference but it looks professional and it can be read easily.)

To replicate the non-fiction example, change the Main Text Style font to Garamond 13. This is one point up from the fiction formatting because I use a larger page size for non-fiction.

3 This will change your font for all future projects but to make the changes to your existing document, select Documents/Convert/Convert formatting to Default Text Style...

4 For non-fiction, I also use a title font of Century Gothic, lead titles being 18pts and sub-titles at 14. I make these changes within the document itself.

Title Page image

I like to include a reflection of the cover font for the title on the interior front page, as in my example here. I achieve this by simply inserting an image in the way I describe in Section 2 - Inserting Images.

I'll discuss the other pages which make up the front matter and the back matter in the next few chapters.

Chapter images

It's the small details that will lift your book above the norm and create a professional looking product. An example, which is simple to include, is a recurring image at the beginning of each chapter. This can be a scroll, a star, a swirl, a cross, something a little more imaginative, anything really.

You add it in by simply following the steps on how to insert any image. (You can find this here) Don't forget though that the more complicated the image, the larger your file will become and the more expensive it will be to distribute.

Font consistency

After you've finished preparing your manuscript, I always look for any font discrepancies, by highlighting large portions of text and double-checking the font.

Smart quotes

'Smart Quote' is the name given to the curly apostrophe as opposed to 'Straight Quote' which is the straighter alternative. The curly version looks more professional and is more interesting on the page. Remember, it's the small details that count. In order to double check that Scrivener has treated all apostrophes the same:

1 Select Format/Convert/Quotes to Smart Quotes

Front Matter

The Front Matter of a book is the name given to the pages at the beginning before you get to the main content.

In order to give you a comprehensive list of the pages included, I've sourced this from www.thebookdesigner.com, who in turn has looked at the industry norm, The Chicago Manual of Style. Bear in mind though, there is no book which actually has all of these pages included. The list is simply here to be used to make sure that you have the right information, in the right sections and the pages are in the right order.

Taken from Joel Friedlander at The Book Designer.com.

"The (front matter refers to) pages at the beginning of a book before the body of the book. These pages are traditionally numbered with lowercase roman numerals."

Half Title
Also called the Bastard title, this page contains only the title of the book and is typically the first page you see when opening the cover. This page and its verso (the back, or left-hand reverse of the page) are often eliminated in an attempt to control the length of the finished book.

Frontispiece An illustration on the verso facing the title page.

Title Page Announces the title, subtitle, author and publisher of the book. Other information that may be found on the title page can include the publisher's location, the year of publication, or descriptive text about the book, and illustrations are also common on title pages.

Copyright Page Usually the verso of the title page, this page carries the copyright notice, edition information, publication information, printing history, cataloging data, legal notices, and the books ISBN or identification number. In addition, rows of numbers are sometimes printed at the bottom of the page to indicate the year and number of the printing. Credits for design, production, editing and illustration are also commonly listed on the copyright page.

In the eBook format, I would include the Copyright page at the back of the book instead, in order to capitalise on the free sample which is often available online.

Below is an example of a simple Copyright page which I use myself:

Copyright © 2013 by Michael J Holley (Smashwords Edition)

All rights reserved. This book or any portion thereof, in both printed or electronic form, may not be reproduced or used in any manner whatsoever without the express written permission of the publisher except for the use of brief quotations in a book review.

All characters, organisations and locations appearing in this work are fictitious. Any resemblance to real persons, living or dead, is purely coincidental.
ISBN 978-0-9575842-4-2

Cover illustration by James at GoOnWrite.com

First published in the United Kingdom in 2013 (1)

Beach Hut Publishing
Cowes
Isle of Wight

www.michaeljholley.com

I also create a secondary Copyright page for Smashwords. I'll explain the importance of this later but you'll need a Copyright page which holds the text '(Smashwords Edition)'. (Written above in red)

Dedication Not every book carries a dedication but, for those that do, it follows the copyright page.

Epigraph An author may wish to include an epigraph - a quotation - near the front of the book. The epigraph may also appear facing the Table of Contents, or facing the first page of text. Epigraphs can also be used at the heads of each chapter.

Table of Contents Also known as the Contents page, this page lists all the major divisions of the book including parts, if used, and chapters. Depending on the length of the book, a greater level of detail may be provided to help the reader navigate the book.

Scrivener can automatically produce a table of contents based on the sections within the Binder. The next chapter explains how to do this.

List of Figures In books with numerous figures (or illustrations) it can be helpful to include a list of all figures, their titles and the page numbers on which they occur.

List of Tables Similar to the List of Figures above, a list of tables occurring in the book may be helpful for readers.

Foreword Usually a short piece written by someone other than the author, the Foreword may provide a context for the main work. Remember that the Foreword is always signed, usually with the author's name, place and date.

Preface Written by the author, the Preface often tells how the book came into being, and is often signed with the name, place and date, although this is not always the case.

Acknowledgments The author expresses their gratitude for help in the creation of the book.

Introduction The author explains the purposes and the goals of the work, and may also place the work in a context, as well as spell out the organisation and scope of the book.

Prologue In a work of fiction, the Prologue sets the scene for the story and is told in the voice of a character from the book, not the author's voice.

Second Half Title If the front matter is particularly extensive, a second half title identical to the first, can be added before the beginning of the text. The page following is usually blank but may contain an illustration or an epigraph. When the book design calls for double-page chapter opening spreads, the second half title can be used to force the chapter opening to a left-hand page.

In order to add each page into the Binder within Scrivener:

1 Right click at the top of the manuscript and Add/New Text. A new page will appear below which you can format as you wish.

Adding a Contents Page

Within Scrivener, it's possible to automatically generate a Table of Contents to add into the Front Matter of your book.

1 Add a folder and a text file by right-clicking in the appropriate area of the Binder, calling it 'Contents'.

2 Highlight which folders or text files you would like to appear in your Table of Contents.

3 Right-click when they are highlighted and select Edit/Copy Special/Copy Documents as ToC.

4 Click into the new text file which you have just created called 'Contents', then select Edit/Paste. The Table of Contents will appear.

5 Be sure to update the Table of Contents, if you adjust the structure later, by repeating the steps above.

Back Matter

The Back Matter of a book is the name given to the pages you see at the end after the main content.

In order to give you a comprehensive list of the pages included, I've sourced this from www.thebookdesigner.com, who in turn has used the industry norm, The Chicago Manual of Style. Once again, bear in mind that there is no book which actually has all of these pages included. The list is simply here to be used to make sure that you have the right information, in the right sections and the pages are in the right order.

Taken from Joel Friedlander at The Book Designer.com.

"At the end of the book various citations, notes and ancillary material are gathered together into the back matter."

Postscript

From the latin post scriptum, "after the writing" meaning anything added as an addition or afterthought to the main body of the work.

Appendix A supplement of some kind to the main work. An Appendix might include source documents cited in the text, material that arose too late to be included in the main body of the work, or any of a number of other insertions.

Chronology In some works, particularly histories, a chronological list of events may be helpful for the reader. It may appear as an appendix, but can also appear in the front matter if the author considers it critical to the reader's understanding of the work.

Notes Endnotes come after any appendices, and before the bibliography or list of references. The notes are typically divided by chapter to make them easier to locate.

Glossary An alphabetical list of terms and their definitions, usually restricted to some specific area.

Bibliography A systematic list of books or other works such as articles in periodicals, usually used as a list of works that have been cited in the main body of the work, although not necessarily limited to those works.

List of Contributors

A work by many authors may demand a list of contributors, which should appear immediately before the index, although it is sometimes moved to the front matter.

Contributor's names should be listed alphabetically by last name, but appear in the form "First Name Last Name." Information about each contributor may include brief biographical notes, academic affiliations, or previous publications.

Index

An alphabetical listing of people, places, events, concepts, and works cited along with page numbers indicating where they can be found within the main body of the work.

Errata

A notice from the publisher of an error in the book, usually caused in the production process.

Colophon

A brief notice at the end of a book usually describing the text typography, identifying the typeface by name along with a brief history. It may also credit the book's designer and other persons or companies involved in its physical production.

Additional Pages for Self-Publishers

Review Page This is increasingly popular amongst self-publishers. When a reader has reached the end of your book, it's a great time to gently remind them to leave a review back on the site where they originally purchased it. Within the eBook format, I would attach live links to make it as easy as possible. Reviews really do make a difference to a book's success and the more you can encourage them the better.

About the Author Take a moment to give the reader a little bit about yourself. Don't drone on for three pages, but something personal might make a fan out of a reader.

Other Books Similar to the review request, the end of your book is a great time to then push your other works in front of the reader. Hopefully, they've just enjoyed the book and are interested to read more. You should have a page per book, including links to major online retailers (eBook only).

In order to add each page into the Binder within Scrivener:

1 Right click at the top of the manuscript and Add/New Text. A new page will appear below which you can format as you wish.

5

Cover Design

Cover Design

If for some reason you've turned straight to this page, without reading any of the rest of the book, then let me reiterate the importance of quality.

Self-publishing now means that you can do everything a traditional publisher does, but better. So, it's important to know that traditional publishers employ professional cover designers to design their books covers. You should too.

Books are sold on the strength of their cover - Fact.

Obviously, there's word-of-mouth, reviews, blurbs, strength of writing, etc., all of which are important but the most important aspect of book marketing is the cover.

You have about two-seconds to pull someone in or allow them to wander off. In that time period, most readers will make a subconscious judgement on the following questions:

- Which genre is it?
- What's the quality of the writing like?
- Is it traditionally published or not?
- Does it sound interesting?
- Does the title match the image?

- Can they read the title?
- Who's the author?
- Does the image pique the curiosity?
- Does it look appealing?
- Does it look similar to other books which the reader likes?
- Is it part of a series?

I'm sure there are even more questions which are answered within this two-second timeframe, but you get the point. The cover is, without a shadow of a doubt, the most important aspect of your book's marketing.

The last thing you want is for your book to look like a school project. You've just spent ages on the writing. It's taken you months, maybe even years, to complete so don't just stick any old thing on it. It would be like wrapping the Mona Lisa in litter.

Don't waste your time thinking that you can do better, even if you're a graphic designer, let a professional book designer work on it for you. Once upon a time this would've been hard but, as the industry changes, there are now affordable design services available to the individual self-publisher. It's up to you how much you spend but, you can spend as little as $30 for a professional design which is already there, you just have to buy it off the shelf.

Market research

The first thing you should do, before anything else, is to have a look in the genre in which you're writing and take some ideas. See what you think works and what doesn't. This is an important part of the process, so make sure that you fully research the market and clearly understand what the successful books have in common. This exercise will then be used to inform the rest of the process.

After completing the research, you have two choices. You can either choose a ready-made cover or, work with a professional cover designer on a bespoke design.

Ready-made covers

These are great for self-published authors who just want something to look good without spending too much money.

They range from $30 to over $100 but, the beauty of a ready-made cover is that it's available immediately. You can simply find ready-made covers by searching the internet on the search term 'Ready-Made Book Covers'. You'll find loads of directories which you can scrawl through and find something which is fitting. I've also included a list at the back of this book with some of the finest.

These are easy, cheap and fast. If you just want your book to *not* look like a school project, then this is the option for you.

Bespoke covers

If, however, you decide that you want a cover which talks directly to your story then you may need to go down the bespoke design route. But, this still doesn't mean that you'll have to re-mortgage your house for it.

1. Finding a designer

Now, a good designer can be found anywhere, but there are some obvious places to begin looking. During your market research, take down the names of any designers whose work you like. Unfortunately, some of these may be out of your price range but, on the other hand, there may well be some who seem affordable and approachable.

Apart from using your market research, you can also search the internet, use social media, canvas opinion on your blog, walk in to your book shop and have a look around. The key to all of this is to know what you want first of all and then, to look for whose style meets your requirements. It's no good having a sci-fi illustrator designing your romance novel. (Unless it's set in space!!)

2. The Brief

The next step is to explain to the designer exactly what you're looking for. This is usually called the Brief. Detailed below is an example of the type of information you would typically need to provide to a designer:

- Book Title
- Author's Name
- Subtitle/Tagline
- Format Required (ebook/paperback)
- Cover Size
- A Brief Synopsis of Book
- Existing Cover ideas
- Examples of similar style covers
- An extract or complete version of book
- Genre
- Target Audience
- Main themes of project
- Backcover Blurb
- Spine Width
- Publisher Logo

3. Communicate

It's a good idea to be as clear as possible with regard to the brief to reduce the risk of surprise, but also it's important to communicate deadline, how many revisions you're allowed and the exact requirements that you have for the eventual format that it's delivered back to you in.

Communication is a two-way street though, and I would think carefully before contracting a designer who goes silent.

Format

Here are the following file formats that you'll need for the various distribution outlets.

eBook
- a .jpeg file of just the front cover.
- 2,820 pixels by 4,500 pixels (ratio 1:1.6)
- high resolution

Paperback
- a .pdf file of the full sleeve, including spine
- high resolution
- Appropriate bleed margins

Title Page Image - a .jpeg image reflecting the font deployed on the front cover. (Not essential, but advised)

6

Creating a Product Description

Creating a Product Description

As soon as your potential reader has been enticed by the cover, the next place they look is the product description (or Blurb). This is the short description on the back of the book, or the Product Description on a book retailer's website.

The purpose of this product description is to make your book sound as appealing as possible. This isn't an exercise in creative writing, this is an exercise in copywriting. Your description must sell your book. However, similar to other aspects of a book, this is subjective but here are some guidelines which should point you in the right direction.

1. Compare the market

Look around at the other books in the same genre. How do their blurbs compare? Is there a genre norm which should be adhered to? Notice the blurbs which have the most impact and decide what works well. Traditional publishers employ blurb specialists, so look at what they produce in your genre and decide on what style works best.

2. Size and structure

When you've found some examples of best practice, notice how many paragraphs they have, how many strap lines appear above or below, how long are they?

3. Focus on the protagonist

Obviously, this applies more to fiction. It's usual for the main characters to be named and characterised in some way. It's important to evoke some emotion within the reader, because if they care about the character then they will be more inclined to read further.

4. Plight

What's going to happen to your protagonist in order for there to be a story in the first place? What's at stake? What can they win or lose?

5. Hope

What chance do they have of being successful? A glimmer of hope works better than if it was a foregone conclusion.

6. Setting

Give a clue as to whether it's set in space, the sea or Arkansas.

7. Who is it for?

Especially for non-fiction, explain who your perfect reader is.

8. What can they learn?

Again for non-fiction, there has to be a point to your book and the reader should usually learn something which they didn't know before.

9. Style

It's a good idea to write the blurb in a similar style to the rest of the book. If it's funny then be funny, if it's dark then be dark. Again, look at other books in the genre and get a feel for what's expected.

10. Draft a 1st version

Just like the rest of the book, it's unlikely that you're going to nail it first time. Allow yourself the freedom of knowing that it's just a draft.

11. Canvas opinion

Show the 1st draft to friends and family, editors and beta-readers. Get their opinion and make any necessary adjustments.

12. Re-write, Review and Re-write again

Keep tweaking until it's as short as possible whilst still packing in the maximum amount of potency. One of the telltale signs of bad self-publishing is a book with about eight paragraphs squeezed on to the back page. It doesn't look good and you'll lessen your chance of a reader actually bothering to start it in the first place. Also, because of the brief window of attention, what you say at the beginning has to be intriguing enough to lead the reader on to the next part, and so on.

13. Testimonials

There's also an opportunity to mention some high level reviews in this space. Again though, keep them brief and only include them if they're from someone who may be known by the potential reader already. Don't tell us what your mate Kevin thought about it.

7

ISBNs

ISBNs

What is an ISBN?

An International Standard Book Number (ISBN) is the unique identifier which is used around the world to record books in print. It is compulsory for any book published in its physical form to be attached to an ISBN. It's also necessary to have an ISBN number in order to publish an ebook to Apple and Kobo.

Separate ISBNs must be allocated to each format of the same book. So, for example, if you have a paperback, an ebook and an audiobook, then you would need three different ISBNs. Strictly speaking, you would also need separate ISBNs for the different formats of ebooks (.mobi and .epub), but many self-published authors just use one number for multiple ebook formats.

The ISBN is the number which is depicted for scanners by the barcode on the back of the book.

If you decide to buy an ISBN number then you must purchase it. There is only one authorised retailer of ISBN numbers within each country and you must pay the price they set.

Here is a list of countries and the corresponding agency they each have:

Country	Agency	Website
United States	Bowker	http://www.isbn.org
United Kingdom & Ireland	Nielsen	http://www.isbn.nielsenbook.co.uk
Australia	Thorpe Bowker	http://www.myidentifiers.com.au
Canada	Canadian ISBN Agency	http://www.collectionscanada.gc.ca
India	Raja Rammohun Roy National Agency for ISBN	anilprabha.isbn@gmail.com
Russia	Russian ISBN Agency	http://www.bookchamber.ru
Brazil	Brazilian ISBN Agency	http://www.isbn.bn.br
France	AFNIL	http://www.afnil.org
Germany	SBN-Agentur für die Bundesrepublik Deutschland	http://www.german-isbn.de
Sweden	Swedish ISBN Agency	http://www.kb.se/isbn
New Zealand	ISBN Agency	http://www.natlib.govt.nz

It is common for ISBNs to be sold in packages of 10, 100 or 1,000.

Do you need one

There is a wealth of conflicting advice and information regarding ISBNs within the new world of self-publishing.

Benefits

- You own the publishing imprint of your book. - This isn't that amazing; it doesn't have anything to do with the content or Intellectual Property because you own that anyway.
- By owning your own ISBN you aren't tied to any one publisher/distributor. - You are required to have an ISBN for print books and CreateSpace will provide one to you with a downside that you can only use it with them. If you ever want to change then you would need to get another ISBN.
- Smashwords will provide you with an ISBN if you publish through their distribution, however, you will not be able to use this elsewhere, and Smashwords will be named as your publishing imprint. Therefore, owing your own will avoid this.
- Amazon will provide you with an ASIN code for free but, again, you will not be able to use this elsewhere. Owning your own will avoid this as well.
- If you have an ISBN, your book can be sold in bookshops.
- If you have an ISBN, your book can be added to libraries.

- Your book can be searched for by its ISBN.
- Your paperback will carry a barcode which will make it appear the same as any other book.

Drawbacks

- They are expensive given that effectively you're only buying a number.

    In the US, 1 = $125, 10 = $275, 100 = $575
    In the UK, 10 = £132 or £78*, 100 = £318 or £264*
    (* lower price if you have purchased before)

- They are unnecessary if you are only selling online.

Conclusion

If you are going to write several books and plan on selling them physically and electronically, then my advice would be to buy a package of ISBNs.

If you only want to write and sell eBooks online then use Amazon's and Smashwords' free alternatives.

8

Compiling the Manuscript

Compiling an eBook File

Once you've completed all of the other steps, you're then ready to actually make your book. We'll start with creating the eBook.

The two files we will produce by the end of this chapter are:

1. A .mobi file (Amazon Kindle Format)
2. An .epub file (Other eBook Format)

1 Select File/Compile... or the icon at the top with the blue arrow, 'Compile for export or print'.

2 In the 'Format As' drop down at the top, choose E-book. I start with this as a base and then make tweaks from here.

3 You're now going to work down the 'Compilation Options' on the left-hand side and first up is 'Contents'.

4 Within 'Contents' you'll find a version of the 'Binder' you've been using for your project. First of all, tick all of the boxes in the 'Include' column which you wish to include. Don't forget to uncheck the Smashwords Copyright page (mentioned here).

5 Secondly, ensure that you tick the 'Pg Break Before' column for each section that you wish to start on a new page, i.e., beginnings of chapters.

6 Lastly, on the 'Contents' tab, tick the As-Is box for any sections which you want to maintain the formatting of. For my fictional novels, I tend to leave most of these blank because I will handle formatting later on in the compile, however, if you have a large amount of specific formatting (i.e., non-fiction) then it may be best to keep it As-Is.

Remember that ebooks remove a lot of formatting when they are created, so any desired look will need to be checked in the Review stage.

7 On the Separators tab, make sure they are all set to 'Empty line'.

8 On the Cover tab, select the cover which you previously uploaded to the 'Binder'. It should be in the drop down box already. If it isn't, then it means that your cover image has not been uploaded correctly.

9 In the Formatting tab, firstly highlight the top Level 1+. I remove the tick from the Title box and also the one below. I do this because I prefer not to have my chapters beginning with the same title that I've labelled the folder with in the 'Binder'. If you do, then experiment with it in.

10 Next, select Section Layout beneath and then Title Prefix and Suffix. This refers to the formatting of your chapter numbers. I prefer to have a number on its own, if you prefer to have text, as above, then ignore this step.

To have just a number on its own, delete the word Chapter and change the 't' in the brackets to an 'n'.

(Note: if you want an elaborate number to appear or a specific wording then you are better putting those into the main document and choosing As-Is in the contents tab)

11 I also prefer to change the padding of each new chapter. This refers to how many lines are left blank before the text comes in on new chapter pages. You can do this by adjusting the number of lines where it says Page Padding on the right hand-side. I choose six lines.

12 Next we have to highlight the bottom line in the Section Type area. It's the one that has a tick in the Text column. This is our main text level. Click on Options and tick 'Remove first paragraph indents' - 'At the start of each new document'.

Within the Section Layout, you can capitalise the first few words of each chapter by selecting the First Page tab. I always choose the first 4 words.

Remember: changing the particular font we use for ebooks is pointless due to eReaders changing the font anyway. Ignore the font when creating ebook files.

13 On the Title Adjustments tab, I want to make sure that I'm not going to have a chapter number on the pages before or after the main story. I can do this by clicking on the settings wheel next to 'Do not add title prefix or suffix to documents'. Then simply tick those pages that you wish not to be included.

14 I don't change anything else in any of the other tabs, but I do make sure that the appropriate information is on the Meta-Data tab.

15 Finally, you must select 'Kindle eBook (.mobi)' in the 'Compile For' drop down. The first time you do this you will need to download KindleGen from the Amazon website. KindleGen is essential in order to format the eBook file to KDP's specifications. A link will appear within the Compile window and all you must do is choose where to save the downloaded file and follow the on-screen instructions.

16 Click Compile. When saving, denote it being a Kindle version in the file title and you have finally created the .mobi file which will be used to upload to Kindle Direct Publishing (KDP).

But, you're not done there. It's just as easy to produce the .epub file at the same time.

17 Again, select File/Compile… or the icon at the top with the blue arrow, 'Compile for export or print'.

18 Select 'ePub eBook (.epub)' in the 'Compile For' drop down list.

19 In the 'Contents' tab, deselect the original Copyright page in the 'Include' column and select the Smashwords Copyright page instead.

20 Click Compile and you have created the .epub file which will be used to upload to Smashwords.

Reviewing an eBook File

There are two types of eBook file to produce if you choose to have your books sold on all the main retailing websites:

1. A .mobi file is required solely for Amazon Kindle
2. An .epub file is required for everything else

Once you've created these files, it's a good idea to review them for formatting errors and to make sure that you're happy with the way they've turned out. If you've followed my advice in the Compile section then these should be minimal but, it's always a good idea to double-check.

Reviewing the .mobi file

Thankfully, Amazon has provided a tool just for this purpose. The aptly named Kindle Previewer. Not only does it review the Kindle file but, you may have noticed that all of the Kindles are slightly different in size and resolution, and this software enables you to check how your book will look across all of these different devices.

In order to use the Kindle Previewer, you must first download it on to your computer for free. Search on "Kindle Previewer Download" and follow the instructions to download it.

Once it's installed, open up Kindle Previewer and follow these steps.

1 Open the .mobi file in the Kindle Previewer which you have just compiled in Scrivener

2 It will open up in the device that it's set to on the homepage of the previewer. You can change these device views either across the toolbar at the top, or by clicking into Devices in the Menu bar and selecting a different view.

3 Use the arrows in the toolbar at the top to move through the book, checking that everything looks as it should.

4 If you find an error, something which doesn't look quite right, then click on the Home icon in the toolbar.

5 Go back into Scrivener, and depending on what needs to be changed, either open the Compile window and make any necessary changes there, or make changes in the manuscript before re-compiling.

6 Compile again in Scrivener, replacing the previous version and then once again, open it up in Kindle Previewer.

7 Repeat steps 3-6 until you're happy with the result.

8 Congratulations, you now have a beautiful Kindle file of your very own which you can be proud of.

Reviewing the .epub file

1 If you have made changes to your .mobi file in the section above, then I would re-compile another .epub file from Scrivener as well.

2 I then use a good .epub previewer which I download for free called Calibre.

Go to (www.calibre-ebook.com)

However, due to the changes that you've already made to the .mobi file, this should only be for peace of mind.

3 Once you're happy with the way that both formats are appearing, you're now ready to start uploading the files on to the distribution sites.

Compiling a Paperback File

You've created the ebook files so you already know your way around the Compile section of Scrivener, but in order to create a paperback file you need to have a much keener eye on the formatting. As explained in the previous chapters, most of the formatting is irrelevant for ebooks but, for paperbacks, we have to put our typography hats on.

We want every page to look good, and this includes;

1. fonts
2. indents
3. spacing
4. margins
5. alignment

Before we get started, the settings I'm going to suggest will produce either; the fiction or the non-fiction design examples which are shown at the beginning of Section 4.

All of this formatting is subjective and, a quick look in a handful of books will show you that, even traditional publishers have their own preferences. However, as a rule, it's best not to let your formatting be another outlet for your expression. The weirder your interior looks, the more it will drive your reader away.

Save as a different document

After you've finished compiling the ebooks, save that final version in Scrivener indicating that it was the final ebook version. I would then save the file again, this time indicating that it's going to be the paperback version.

Fonts

Run through your front and back matter making sure that you're using the same font for them and that they're looking as they're meant to. For all of my fiction I use Garamond 12 and for non-fiction I use Garamond 13.

Double check the Front and Back Matter ensuring that the alignment and fonts are consistent.

Double check the Smart Quotes as well. You can find out how to do that in Section 4.

Indents

There are two main types of indent; 1) the first line indent, and 2) all subsequent indents, known as hanging indents. Review your manuscript to make sure that all of your indents are consistent throughout.

1 To change an indent, place the cursor in the appropriate place and select Format/Text/Increase/Decrease Indents

Line Spacing

I like to use a line spacing of 1.2 because I think it makes it easier to read. Of course, this is once again a personal preference and I encourage you to try all of these settings to find the perfect look for you.

1 Highlight the entire document, excluding any front or back matter which may require different line spacing.

2 Go to Format/Text/Line and Paragraph Spacing..., and adjust the Line Height Multiple. (or adjust in the drop-down list at the top of the screen)

Margins

To ensure that the margins are set correctly for your manuscript, you need to go back into the Page Setup and check your page settings. You can remind yourself of how to do this in Section 4.

Alignment

Make sure that your text is justified towards each margin.

1 Highlight the entire document, excluding any front or back matter which may require different alignment.

2 Go to Format/Text/Justify. (or click on the icon at the top)

Compile

1 Select File/Compile... or the icon at the top with the blue arrow, 'Compile for export or print'.

2 In the 'Compile For' drop down at the bottom, choose PDF.

3 Within the 'Contents' page, remember to set a page break before each chapter and, I also like to set the front and back matter to 'As-Is' as I've just checked that the fonts are all right. By keeping them 'As-is', I ensure that the indentations, etc., all remain the same. If you have any different looking chapters, it may be worth keeping those 'As-Is' as well.

4 Within 'Print Settings' always keep as Publishing.

5 On the Separators tab, make sure they are all set to 'Empty line'.

6 In the Formatting tab, make sure that the 'Override text and notes formatting' box is ticked at the top and then highlight the top Level 1+. I remove the tick from the Title box and also the one below. I do this because I prefer not to have my chapters beginning with the same title that I've labelled the folder with in the 'Binder'. If you do, then experiment with it in.

7 Next, select Section Layout beneath and then Title Prefix and Suffix. This refers to the formatting of your chapter numbers. I prefer to have a number on its own, if you prefer to have text, as above, then ignore this step.

To have just a number on its own, delete the word Chapter and change the 't' in the brackets to an 'n'. You should be left with 1.

(Note: if you prefer an elaborate number to appear or a specific wording then you are better putting those into the main document and choosing As-Is in the contents tab)

8 I also prefer to change the padding of each new chapter. This refers to how many lines are left blank before the text comes in on new chapter pages. You can do this by adjusting the number of lines where it says Page Padding on the right hand-side. I choose six lines.

9 Next we have to highlight the bottom line in the Section Type area. It's the one that has a tick in the Text column. This is our main text level.

10 Firstly, change the formatting of the font used for the body of your book here. Click on the capital A above the sample text and, in my case, I change it to Garamond 12. I also change the line spacing to 1.2. This affects any pages which are not 'As-Is'.

11 Click on Options and tick 'Remove first paragraph indents' - 'At the start of each new document'.

12 Within the Section Layout, you can capitalise the first few words of each chapter by selecting the First Page tab. I always choose the first 4 words.

Note: if you've selected As-Is on the contents tab then numbers 6-12 will be irrelevant.

13 On the Title Adjustments tab, I want to make sure that I'm not going to have a chapter number on the pages before or after the main story. I can do this by clicking on the settings wheel next to - 'Do not add title prefix or suffix to documents'. Then simply tick those pages that you don't want included.

14 The next set of adjustments are on the 'Page Settings' tab. Firstly, tick the 'Use project Page Setup settings' box at the top. If you have not set your page settings yet, then look back at Section 4.

15 Also, on the Page Settings tab, you can create the professional looking headers and footers which you're used to seeing in paperbacks. I prefer to put the book title in the top right-hand corner and my name in the top left-hand corner. Page numbers should mirror these at the bottom.

Here are the settings:

Header and Footer tab

> Header, Right-Hand Side, Book Name
> Footer, Right-Hand Side, <$p>

16 On the First Pages tab, you must select 'Different first pages header/footer' to prevent page numbers and headers appearing on beginning of chapter pages.

17 Also, on the First Pages tab, you must calculate on which page you want your header and footer to begin. It's not customary to have a header and a footer as part of the front matter.

18 On the Facing Pages tab, I tick the 'Use facing pages' box and enter the following settings:

> Header, Left-Hand Side, Book Name
> Footer, Left-Hand Side, <$p>

19 I then set the Header font to Optima Regular 9 and Footer font to Optima Regular 11.

20 Lastly, I make sure that the appropriate information is on the Meta-Data tab.

21 Click Compile. When saving, denote it being the paperback version in the file title and you have finally created the .pdf file which will be the interior of your paperback.

Reviewing a Paperback File

You should now have a .pdf file of your book in the directory in which you saved it. It's now time to scan through it and check for any mistakes. Unfortunately, there's no easy, straight-forward shortcut for this but there may be smarter ways to achieve it than others.

1 Open your .pdf file in whichever application you prefer. I use either Adobe Reader or the native Preview app on Mac.

2 In Adobe Reader, I switch to the Thumbnails view and drag it, so it stretches across the whole screen. In Preview, select View/Contact Sheet. Either way, you want to end up with a page view of your book as inch square thumbnails.

3 Scan through the entire book and check for any issues. You're looking for images which are severed from the text they relate to by sitting on the next page, or a chapter which starts halfway down a page inconsistent with the other chapters, or the very end of a paragraph sitting at the top of a clean page. All of these problems will just look strange and you'll see them immediately.

As a rule of thumb, if there are only two lines at the top of a page then I look to adjust the previous page so that I can squeeze them on. I tend to fall back on two methods to achieve this; I either tweak the line spacing minimally or, I adjust the font size. Neither of these are very pleasant and I make sure that I adjust the text just enough to solve the issue without going over the top.

4 To make these changes, go back into Scrivener and make the necessary adjustment to the relevant page. This is a trial and error, iterative process and you won't know if you've solved it fully until you re-compile and check the .pdf file again.

Note: You need to make sure that you've ticked the option to Preserve Line Spacing within the Compile section. This way you can make changes and they will be taken into account when compiling.

5 Keep repeating steps 3 and 4 until the entire document is just the way it should be.

6 You also need to make sure that any single pages start on the right-hand side of the book. (For example, Title Page, Dedication Page, First Chapter, Acknowledgments, etc.) If they don't, then you will need to go back into Scrivener and insert a single blank text file into the relevant area of the binder. Don't forget to include this page in the Compile before checking it again.

Here is a checklist of the items you need to look for when scanning your book.

- Widows and Orphans
- Line indentations
- Unexpected changes of font
- Correct page placement (pagination)
- Images
- Front and Back Matter
- Headers and Footers

Remember, all of this is important. If you're going to be selling physical copies then this is what your reader will see way before they read about what you have to say. It has to look professional.

9

Publishing the EBook

Publishing to Amazon

Amazon's Kindle is by far the most popular eReader in the world. In the UK, figures from May 2013 claimed that 79% of all ebooks sold were bought from Amazon. In the US, the figure is nearer 65%, but it's clear to see that Amazon is by far the biggest ebook retailer in the world. So, you need your book available on Kindle.

Thankfully, it's quite straightforward if you've followed my advice up until now. Let's take a look at the files you'll need before you start thinking about publishing.

1. Kindle .mobi file

This is the file which was exported from Scrivener in the 'Compiling Your eBook File' section. It's your finished book. It has a cover included and all of your beautiful formatting.

2. Cover in .jpeg or .tif file

You should have received this from your cover designer. It will be in the exact format that KDP requires. Let's take a look at those requirements again:

- For best quality, 2,820 pixels on the shortest side
- 4,500 pixels on the longest side
- High resolution
- RGB colour mode

With these two files in your possession, you're ready to publish on to Amazon.

Kindle Direct Publishing (KDP)

Kindle Direct Publishing, or KDP, is the name given to the Amazon website in which you submit your ebook for publication. You access it in the same way as you access any other website.

www.kdp.amazon.com

1 Register an account, or sign in using your Amazon account.

2 Click on Add New Title

Submission Process

1. Enter Your Book Details

    o   Book name
    o   Subtitle
    o   Is this book part of a series?
    o   Edition Number
    o   Publisher
    o   Description
    o   Book contributors
    o   Language
    o   ISBN

2. Verify Your Publishing Rights

Here you need to verify whether you have the necessary publishing rights. If you wrote it, then you do. Below is the definition from Amazon:

"Publishing rights are the rights you need to publish a book. To publish a book for Kindle through KDP, you must have obtained all rights necessary to publish the digital book from the book's author and any other content creators, or, if you are the book's author, you must have retained all of the necessary digital book publishing rights.

"If you are publishing a public domain book, keep in mind that the duration of copyright varies between countries, so ensure that you indicate your territory rights accurately. (If your book is in the public domain in one country but not another, you must identify your territory rights accordingly.) Books that consist entirely or primarily of public domain content are not eligible for the 70% royalty option. For full details, terms and conditions see the Pricing page and Terms and Conditions.

"If your book is under copyright and you hold the necessary rights for this content, select "This is not a public domain work and I hold the necessary publishing rights." If your book is a public domain book, select "This is a public domain work."

3. Target Your Book To Your Customers

- Category (you can choose up to 2)
- Age Range
- US Grade Range
- Search keywords (up to 7)

4. Select Your Book Release Option

You can either choose to release your book immediately, or make it available for pre-order. This enables you to promote your book before the launch date.

5. Upload or Create a Book Cover

This is where you upload the cover design .jpeg image. Don't worry if the thumbnail looks grainy after you've uploaded. It won't look like that when it's on sale.

6. Upload Your Book File

Firstly, you can choose whether you want Digital Rights Management applied to your book. The purpose of DRM is to prevent future sharing of your file as an anti-piracy measure. I've chosen it in the past but I'm not sure if it's the right thing to do or not. This is a personal decision that you'll have to make yourself.

Next, browse for your .mobi file and upload your book. A

confirmation message tells you it's successful.

7. Preview Your Book

If you've already checked your ebook file in the Kindle Previewer then you probably don't need to do this, but it might be worth a quick sanity check.

8. Verify Your Publishing Territories

This is self-explanatory. I always choose 'Worldwide rights'. If you only hold rights within certain regions then this is where you need to flag that up.

9. Set Your Pricing and Royalty

This depends on which pricing strategy you're going for, and you could probably write an entire book on the various pricing models which authors use. Very simply, you can pick a US dollar price and assume a similar price point across all other countries, or you can distinguish between certain countries.

Amazon has now included a helpful graph which will show you the most effective price point for your type of book, however remember that this price point is only effective from a one-book pricing strategy. If you're writing a series, for example, your pricing may be very different across the individual books.

You'll also notice that you can choose between a 35% royalty and a 70% royalty. In order to qualify for the 70% royalty you must set your book price at $2.99 at least.

10. Kindle MatchBook

This function gives you the choice to either opt in or out of the MatchBook program. If you opt in, then you can allow your ebook to be downloadable for either free or $0.99 if a customer purchases a physical copy of your book. Again, this is a purely subjective decision.

11. Kindle Book Lending

You can either allow users to lend your book after purchasing to their friends and family for a duration of 14 days, or not.

12. Save and Publish

Tick the box to confirm that you're happy with the terms and conditions, and then you're ready to

[Save and Publish]

You usually have to wait for about a day before an email confirms that the book is available online.

Congratulations, you're now a published author!!!

Publishing to Smashwords

Smashwords is the online distributor which will forward your ebook to the following retailers:

- Apple
- Kobo
- Barnes & Noble (Nook)
- Scribd
- Oyster
- OverDrive
- Baker & Taylor
- Inktera.com
- Versent.com
- WH Smith (UK)
- Play (UK)
- Flipkart (India)
- FNAC (France & Portugal)
- Livraria Cultura (Brazil)
- Angus & Robertson (Australia)
- Bookworld (Australia)
- Collins (Australia)
- Indigo (Canada)
- Feltrinelli (Italy)

- Libris (Netherlands)
- Paper Plus (New Zealand)
- Whitcoulls (New Zealand)
- Rakuten (Japan)
- Buy.com (US)

It's the easiest, most effective way of submitting your work to the remainder of the non-Amazon world. You submit once and the rest is taken care of.

Go to www.smashwords.com

1 Register an account

2 Click 'Publish' on the blue tool bar

Submission Process

1. Title and synopsis

Enter your book's details, you should be used to this by now.

2. Pricing and sampling

Make sure you enter the same price for an ebook that you entered on KDP, otherwise there'll be a section of your readers who are getting a bum deal.

3. Categorization

Choose the two categories where you have the best chance of finding your readers.

4. Tags

Enter the ten keywords which your readers are most likely to use to find a book like yours.

5. Ebook formats

If you've followed these guidelines then you'll be uploading an .epub file rather than a Word file, so this section can be ignored.

If you are uploading a Word file then I can't see any reason why you wouldn't tick all of them.

6. Cover image

Upload the ebook cover .jpeg file. This is the same file which was used for KDP.

7. Select file of book to publish

This is where you upload the .epub file of the ebook which you compiled earlier from Scrivener.

8. Publishing agreement

Tick the box and hit, Publish.

Congratulations, you're now a published author... again!!!

10
Publishing the Paperback

Publishing to CreateSpace

It's now possible for a self-published author to offer a physical book to their readers without filling up their garage with boxes. Due to the advances in digital publishing and print-on-demand, there are now services available which can print individual books, one at a time, when required.

Out of these print-on-demand companies, I believe that CreateSpace is the simplest to use.

CreateSpace is owned by Amazon and therefore links seamlessly with the eBook title which you've already submitted through KDP. Once you've created both an ebook and a paperback, your listing on Amazon will look like this:

Formats	Amazon Price	New from	Used from
Kindle Edition	£1.97	--	--
Paperback	£5.74	£4.63	£5.96

I'm unsure whether paperbacks are particularly important in the current environment. There are very few places to sell paperbacks because of the reduction in bookshops, and online book sales consist largely of ebooks. However, if we stand by the principle that we want our books to resemble traditionally published books as much as possible, then offering a paperback format adds to the perception. Also, creating a physical book at least gives you something to turn up with if you're attempting to get out there and press the flesh.

So, assuming that you're going to create a paperback, I think CreateSpace is the best way to go. It's the easiest, it's the most effective with regard to Amazon and it's the most competitive with regard to printing costs. However, there are other print-on-demand alternatives which may better suit your particular needs. Scribe is a new service, which offers greater printing capabilities for illustrations and appears to create beautiful looking books.

This area of self-publishing is continually changing due to technical developments and it's worth making sure that you're picking the right option for you.

Submission Process

1. Title Information

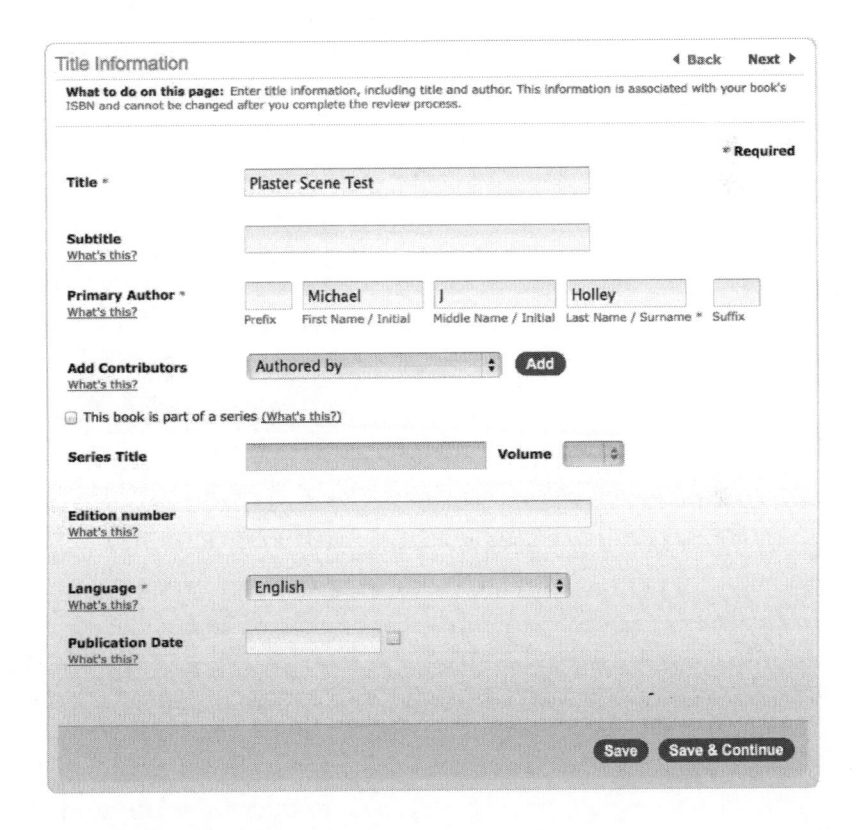

Title Information ◀ Back   Next ▶

What to do on this page: Enter title information, including title and author. This information is associated with your book's ISBN and cannot be changed after you complete the review process.

* Required

Title * Plaster Scene Test

Subtitle
What's this?

Primary Author *   Prefix   First Name / Initial: Michael   Middle Name / Initial: J   Last Name / Surname *: Holley   Suffix
What's this?

Add Contributors   Authored by   [Add]
What's this?

☐ This book is part of a series (What's this?)

Series Title   Volume

Edition number
What's this?

Language * English
What's this?

Publication Date
What's this?

[Save]   [Save & Continue]

2. ISBN

You can either choose to use your own ISBN or a CreateSpace-Assigned ISBN.

If you've decided to purchase an ISBN package for yourself then this is where you'd allocate one to your book. However, an ISBN is not an essential attribute when publishing a book and you can use a CreateSpace-Assigned number if you prefer. Refer to the dedicated section on ISBNs for more details.

3. Interior

This is where you upload the .pdf file which you created in the Scrivener compile. After it's uploaded, you can then check the formatting in the Interior Reviewer application. I definitely recommend that you do this to make sure that every page looks right.

If something looks wrong, you'll have to go right back into Scrivener, make any changes, re-compile, re-check the .pdf file and then upload once again into CreateSpace to check the Interior Reviewer. This can be a trial and error process but ultimately worthwhile.

4. Cover

You can now choose whether you want a matte or glossy cover. Call me old-fashioned but I believe books should have matte covers, otherwise they look like magazines, but it's a preference-thing.

After this decision, all you have to do is upload the .pdf file for your paperback cover. If you've followed the guidelines up until now then this should be straightforward.

5. Complete Setup

Finally, all you have to do is confirm that the information is correct. You can also order a physical proof copy and, I'd recommend you do this just to make sure that it feels right in your hands. You can't beat that feeling of actually holding your own book.

Congratulations, you've now published a physical book too!!

11

Next Steps

Next Steps

Once you've published the book, I suppose this is when the work really begins. Being a self-publisher is about being an entrepreneur. This book has given you the necessary tools to enable you to publish your book but you now need to turn your attention towards marketing and developing your strategy as a writer.

There are marketing specialists who can offer better advice than me in this arena and I will include some of these resources at the back of this book.

However, it depends what your objectives are for self-publishing a book. You could be a fiction writer, looking to begin a new career. The opportunities are there now and you certainly wouldn't be alone. If this is you, then the best advice is to get on with the next book, immediately. The best form of marketing for fiction writers is to keep producing books. Eventually, you will begin to build a brand, a platform, and develop true champions of your work who will spread the word, but this won't happen with one or two books.

Alternatively, your self-published book may be a non-fiction project designed to add credibility to another business. It may be there to facilitate a speaking career, or even to support a specialism in a niche area. If so, then perhaps the one book is enough for your plans. Now you know how to self-publish though, the opportunity is always there in the future to add to your catalogue, reaching out to an even wider audience.

Whatever you decide to do next, at least you can say that you've now published a book and *that* book will be around forever.

Good luck... and keep self-publishing.

Note from the Author

Thank you so much for reading this guide on self-publishing a book. I hope you've enjoyed it and, more importantly, that you've actually used it to self-publish your project.

It would be great if you could tell others about this book in the places you hang out online.

Also, reviews are massively important when selling books, so if you've enjoyed it and found it helpful, then perhaps you would consider leaving a rating and a review on your preferred book retailer site.

More self-publishing tips

Join my mailing list here in order to keep up-to-date with self-publishing news, advice, upcoming books and workshops. Or, take a look at my author website at www.michaeljholley.com.

Author Resources

Self-Publishing Books and Websites

Write, Publish, Repeat - Sean Platt, Johnny B Truant
Fiction Unboxed - Sterling & Stone
Business for Authors - Joanna Penn
Let's Get Digital - David Gaughran
TheCreativePenn.com
TheBookDesigner.com
Jane Friedman
Author Marketing Club

Self-Publishing Podcasts

The Creative Penn
The Self-Publishing Podcast
The Sell More Books Show
The Rocking Self-Publishing Podcast
Self-Publishing Round Table

Professional Cover Design

Go On Write.com
99 Designs
Author Marketing Club
Kit Foster
Jason Gurley
The Book Cover Designer
JD & J
The Cover Collection

Professional Editing

Bubble Cow
Self-Publishing.com
The Fiction Doctor

Acknowledgements

It's great to have the opportunity to thank people at the end of every book I write. Being a full-time writer means that I spend inordinately large amounts of time on my own, staring at a screen or out of the window. It can be an incredibly isolating existence. I create suspended realities and fill them with made up people, who I talk to, regularly. If it wasn't for those other 'real' people who I share my life with and allow me to disappear into my own head, none of my books would have been completed.

So, first of all, I'd like to thank my family, who have supported my entire writing journey, even through the Van Gogh moments. Especially, I want to thank Claire for her patience over the last three years and I promise that life will continue to be all right.

I also want to thank my editor, Lian, for the time that she spends sifting through my waste, somehow crafting a decent product out of it.

I also need to thank my fiction beta-readers who are all friends and are somehow still keen to look through my drafts. Thank you Des, Amanda, Tim and Phil. Special thanks to Fran Heath for reviewing this book.

Finally, I want to thank the hundreds of people who read my blog most days, some of whom take the time to comment and pass on advice. I love writing the blog and sharing my mistakes so that others can learn from them. Without the website, I wouldn't have even considered writing this book so... thank you.

About the Author

Michael J Holley is the author of three comedy novels; Cast in the Summer of Love, The Great Corporate Escape and The Christmas Number One.

His stand-alone stories tend to be funny, plot-driven adventures littered with interesting characters from the real world. They are almost as good for escaping as a hacksaw baked into a Victoria Sponge.

After being born in Southampton, he had spells in Liverpool, Manchester and Stockholm before he realised that an international career in accountancy was finally threatening to destroy his best years. Thankfully, three years ago he upped and moved his family to the Isle of Wight, and ever since has been a full-time writer.

His website, which focuses on indie-publishing, has received over 100,000 views, he has published a guide to self-publishing and is regularly running self-publishing courses across the country.

Having been the taller half of the rhythm section for the indie-rock band Aura4, Michael still enjoys listening to proper music and playing in bands. He also loves watching and playing football, swimming, reading (of course) and drinking good coffee.

You can follow him at:

Twitter (@mjholleywriter)
Facebook (Michael J Holley)
www.michaeljholley.com

CAST IN THE SUMMER OF LOVE

Michael J Holley

Cast in the Summer of Love

1967

The Summer of Love

A brotherhood of man, revolution in the air, and experimental Celia, is way ahead of her time

2013

Time still hasn't caught up with her but now, Celia's about to die

A secret, which she buried nearly 50 years ago, is about to be exposed and it could change the face of rock 'n' roll forever

Love leaves a lasting impression, and sometimes...

...all you need is love

THE GREAT CORPORATE ESCAPE

A NOVEL

Sometimes you just have to take freedom into your own hands

Michael J Holley

The Great Corporate Escape

Ben Jenkins's corporate career is killing him slowly with boredom whilst his boss, Rupert Savage, has the potential to kill him quickly with his bare hands.

It seems as though he has everything; a good job, a loving family and great friends, but the thought of spending the next thirty years in the corporate world is making him desperately, desperately miserable.

He's lost but dreams of escape, and the only refuge he has, is his imagination. The more obsessed he becomes the more his imagination takes hold, until he's only left with one option...

... to take freedom into his own hands.

The Great Corporate Escape is a comedy for anyone who has ever had trouble discovering what's important in their life.

5 FESTIVE VALUE

THE CHRISTMAS NUMBER ONE

And other Christmas Stories

also featuring:
Mistletoe & Wine ✪ Saviour's Day ✪
White Christmas ✪ and at least one more

Michael J Holley

The Christmas Number One
(and other Christmas stories)

This collection of modern short stories occurs during one Christmas and it has a mixture of storytelling styles, which complement the different characters who are included. Michael Holley links each story together with his unique sense of humour and his satirical wit.

"The Christmas Number One" - Two of the most influential players in the music industry go head-to-head for the Christmas Number One.

"Saviour's Day" – A Premiership footballer avoids going to the Children's Hospital with the rest of the team, but his manager forces him to go on his own.

"White Christmas" - Professor Martin Stevenson is isolated in the Arctic Circle at a meteorological station. On Christmas Day he goes for a walk and discovers something that will change his life forever.

"Mistletoe and Wine" - How will family man David Gallagher fare against the persistence and tenacity of the temptress Siobhan when they meet up at the work party?

"Hark! The Herald Angels Sing" - A comical sketch set in heaven, as the Angel System™ is in desperate need of an overhaul.

THE BEGINNER'S GUIDE TO SELF-PUBLISHING A BOOK

A STEP-BY-STEP MANUAL

MICHAEL J HOLLEY

Printed in Great Britain
by Amazon.co.uk, Ltd.,
Marston Gate.